CHANGING HABITS

How to Effectively Form New Habits that
Lead to Success in Life

Daniel Wells

ISBN: 1514161346
ISBN-13: 978-1514161340

DEDICATION

In order to alleviate some of the troubles that bar you
from success, this book examines some academic studies
on discipline, motivation, and habit building.

CONTENTS

INTRODUCTION

Everybody chases success in life, but it is not easy to know what each one of them considers successful. Again, one would wonder if those with low self-esteem share this dream. What about the most ambitious people? Do they want success more than others? The bottom line is there are no ideal parameters for measuring achievement.

However, there are some factors that can come into play. Conventionally, failure or prosperity comes through a person's effort or lack of it. As such, it is fair to deduce that you have complete control of your destiny. In some sobering words, Aristotle once said, "people are what they do in repetition. Then, excellence is a habit, not an act." This statement is a reminder nobody can become successful in an overnight.

It is a procedural activity that gets from one point in life to another. In the modern lives, it is a daunting to build habits because there are several distractions that can lead a person astray. The distractors can get you out of the narrow and straight paths to your old ways of going about things. As the saying goes, perfection is achievable through practice.

In order to alleviate some of the troubles that bar you from success, this book examines some academic studies on discipline, motivation, and habit building. The document also breaks down those findings into various actionable steps that a dedicated habit-builder can practice.

CHAPTER 1 – THE IMPORTANCE OF GOAL-SETTING

Set "micro goals" and "macro objectives."

In a comprehensive study about *Motivation*, a group of scholars discovered that abstract thinking is an effective tool to help with utmost discipline. In the most general sense, "a big dream" is the best equipment to help you start developing the habits that can drive towards success.

Several varieties of research around the theory of *Self-determination* shows that building an intrinsic motivator is a crucial process of building habits that last. People should get motivation to do things by choice, not through rewards or punishments.

Therefore, you should look for ways of balancing your daily activities and desire to dream big. Usually, those dreams do not result in fast, dramatic results. However, there could be a change of things if you develop "*micro quotas"* and *"macro objectives."* Here, your goals are the items of the big picture that you yearn to accomplish. On the other, the quotas symbolize the minimum amounts of tasks that you must do every day to turn your primary objective a reality. They make all your days approachable, and the goals become achievable in return.

A writer and developer, Barry Nathan, made an informative case study of the use of these goals to make things work out. He presented a story of someone who forced himself to write down articles of 100 words per day. He would strive for doing that by avoiding all distractions and writing at all costs.

In the end, the result was impressive. He published three books, which fetched thousands of dollars in the markets. You do not have start from a high level because even the small steps count.

It might seem like a daunting task, but focusing on one goal at a time remains the most intensive way of solving all the problems at hand. The number of targets does not matter, just handle them one after the other. When you take on many of them at one ago, you end up spreading your focus and energy, yet you need all of them for a single goal.

So, how can you deal with five goals if you want to achieve them? Consider the following procedure. Pick the first one and focus on it first. If it is a long-term objective, split it into mini-goals that you can accomplish within the shortest time available, say one month. Pick the first action you can deal with on the first day.

Repeat the same procedure for the entire target. Here, you have to execute one action every day as you pick up one mini-goal after another until the project reaches completion. You must deploy the same criterion for the remaining four goals.

Some activities are run-on, requiring you to set targets as long as they are operational. Examples include visiting the gym or blogging. In that case, you could transform them into habits until you ingrain them into your system. After which, you can focus on the next goal till you exhaust them.

Create Several Chains of Behavior

The secret of creating lasting habits is much easier when you make use of your existing routines than when you try to fight or replace them. The rationale behind the *if-then* planning underlines the environmental factors that you can use to remind yourself to act on your habits.

Widely known as *implementation intentions*, this concept involves using a regular bit of your routine to build a new one. In other words "link it to the chain" of other habits that you form to achieve an objective.

For example, instead of "I will keep my house clean", you could opt for, "I will change my clothes and wash the room/kitchen/ office". Many studies deem this strategy to be a successful way of relying on the contextual cues over a person's willpower. Always, you should opt for "washing all the clothes" when you get the time. That decision is better than, "*If* it is a sunny day, *then* I will only wash the light clothes that need little sunlight to dry."

Eliminate Extra Options

Several studies on self-control like the one available in the book, *The Willpower Effect*, reveal that there is the ultimate power in becoming an irksome person.

For example, take President Obama Barack's insistence on wearing gray and blue suits to work. He said, "I am trying to get the best way to pare decisions down. I do not want to come up with too many decisions about the foods I eat or the clothes I wear. Doing those activities will take up the time I need to make other decisions."

The president's take has the support of a particular research, **Vohs Kathleen and her colleagues'**, on self-control. The study echoes that making repeated choices depletes the mental energy of a person, even if those selections are mundane and very pleasant.

The *Harvard Business Review* affirms that you need to carry out two activities if you are interested in maintaining long-term discipline. You must "Identify all your life aspects that you think mundane" for starters. After which, you 'routinize' them in the best way you deem suitable. In other, do not make very many decisions.

If you aim at achieving a lasting change, you need to understand that the activities you do must both work with your schedule and environment.

For example, you must stop buying junk food if you want to quit them (that requires much use of common sense, not willpower). Similarly, you can eat junk-less meals on a daily basis, and embrace the power of having a routine   that   can   change   health   and   life.

Daniel Wells

CHAPTER 2 - PROCESS PLANNING

Make Process Plans

There is a step that almost everybody skips when fantasizing about building new habits. They never have a direct answer to why they want to adopt a new change in their lives. That answer may seem as an irrelevant detail, but it plays an integral role in boosting your motivation whenever you plan to transform your life. A particular research showed that excess fantasies about some outcomes can become very detrimental to the stickiness of nearly all habits.

According to a study done by UCLA researchers, the mistake is not that you fantasize excessively, but more on what you visualize. The researchers had two groups of people undergo visualization. They found that those who visualized with comprehensible strategies that that they use to reach their goals were likely to remain consistent. In this case, they fantasized about learning French by having to practice every day after their works. On the other hand, their peers did not realize their targets because they did not have strategies. Instead, the visualized themselves travelling to Paris while speaking French. The researchers deduced that the success of that practice stemmed from two factors

- *Proper Planning*:

This preparation mechanism helped the researchers visualize the entire process, helping them to focus their attention on the steps that could lead them to their goal.

- *Emotion*:

The visualization of every step enabled them to reduce excess anxiety.

Eliminate Frustrations

In most cases, the new traits come with drawbacks that lead you astray because they are very fragile. However, it is for that reason that you must eliminate all sources of friction that come your way when you practice new characters. Unless you prepare for such encounters, you may pay much attention to frustrations rather than changes. The "Ouch! What's this!?" moments are the ones that will make you say, "Screw all these, they are not worth my time!" The modern scientists describe this phenomenon as the *What the Hell Effect*.

You are likely to jump out of the ship with new habits at the first slip up if you suffer from this 'ailment.' The good news about it is that this eBook gives you a comprehensive answer to it. Examine and review your habit in efforts to find out where your plans start to fall through. After which, you can improvise ways of making them work rather than dropping the entire strategy that could potentially lead to success. Look at the 99U speaker and author, Sethi Ramit's turnaround to improving his gym attendance. Your focus should go to finding out where his plan would slip up:

When I took time to analyze why my gym attendance was not perfect, I realized that the reason was the fact that I had my closet in another room. So I had to walk through the cold to change into other clothes. I found it easier to stay in my bed and get warmth from the blanket. When I realized that, I started to fold my clothes and shoes the night before the gym session. I would roll over the next morning to see my gym shoes and clothes on the floor when I woke up. The results came my way. My gym attendance improved in the excess of 300%.

Just as Sethi overcame his barrier, you too can get over all the hurdles that bar you from achieving your goals. You can also have another analysis to his story and realize how easy small things can stop you from getting big ones. Sethi feared the morning chill, but that should not worry him so much. He was about to go to the gym where he could sweat and feel warm. With such a mentality, you can cover huge strides in advancing your life and making it successful.

Alternatively, you can also incorporate the "if-then" mechanism when you identify the gaps in your plan. For example, you can use it if fatigue is barring you from playing piano after work. Try "If I feel tired after getting home from the office, then I will take a nap for 20 minutes and play some music for ten minutes to seek motivation." This system will become your habit and improve your piano skills (that is success).

There is no blueprint for creating new traits because whatever you do on a daily basis becomes a habit. However, you need to learn that not all of them bring success. Some just bring failure while others do not change anything in you. What these facts mean is that you a need a 'special' program to practice that one habit that will see achieve some success in life. Once you have a strategy for doing that, things will just work out for you.

Extend your eliminations to the non-essentials that also bar your progress. Here, you must start by identifying the significant things, as well as the ones you love. After which, eliminate the remnants. With the help of this approach, you get the room to focus on the essential activities. Not only does it simplify your tasks, but also works with anything, including projects and life in general.

CHAPTER 3 - THE R'S OF HABIT CHANGE

Prepare Daily Programs

You will find it more manageable to introduce new habits when you create regular plans for the day. Your life can change for the better if you come up with perfect schedules. This tip suggests that best routines come at the start or end of the day, whether it is a workday or not. That approach gives you room to create three routines for the day: one program for the start of the day (work and daily activities), another for the end of your job and duties, and the last one for your evenings.

Unless you have an idea how they can improve your lifestyle, do not just prepare new programs. This mechanism helps you to have a perfect start to the day, and finish it with a preparation for tomorrow. Most importantly, it helps you to firm the roots of productive habits that you plan to nurture in the future. In addition, it also in making sure that you do all tasks you have in a day. There is no doubt that success will "chase" you things can work for you in that manner.

Everybody can start new conventions that stick, but that only happens if they ways of going about that process. In a nutshell, your lifestyle is a depiction of your habits. That is to say that your they will make you in shape, happy, successful or lead you towards the opposite direction. What you do on a regular basis (think and do each day) forms the things you believe in, the person you become, and the personality you will portray. Most importantly, you should develop the interest to improve your habits, create room for adopting new ones, and draw up strategies for achieving them.

This eBook presents a helpful framework that will help you build new conventions, and teach you how to stick to them. As a result, you could see various aspects of your life improve; this includes your health, family, and work. Every habit, whether unpleasant or impressive, follows this conventional tool. For the purpose of this document, use it a productive way that will guide you towards becoming prosperous in your endeavors.

The R's

There are three R's that pertains the change or adoption of a new habit. They include *reminder, routine,* and *reward.* Each of the R's has a specific role to play in the entire process of "becoming a new person". The *reminder* is a trigger that initiates the new behavior; *routine* is a set of actions you take on it; and *reward* is the benefit you get from the change. This framework has undergone several studies by renowned behavioral psychology experts, and as such, it becomes an informative tool that can help you in many ways.

This blueprint presents the works of Fogg B.J. and Duhigg Charles on habit. The latter's best-seller, The Power of Habit, refers to the features of this framework as cue, routine, and reward. Fogg, on the other hand, replaces cue with trigger. All in all, these scholars' analyses are in line with each other. This eBook, however, opts for reminder in efforts to come up with a complement to the other two "R's."

Regardless, the terminologies are not more important (or at least, do not hung up on them) than the information they give. You need to realize that the habit formation process in this framework is rich in science. That scientific knowledge is the same one that your habits follow.

A Demonstration

Take a look at a typical habit that you do on a daily basis and incorporates this criteria. An example here would include eating

1. You get hungry (reminder). The feeling (or yawning) becomes the initiator of the behavior that you undertake. The hunger acts as a cue or reminder that tells you to eat something. Therefore, the prompt will start the routine.

2. You get some food to eat (routine). This becomes the typical behavior. When you become hungry, you look for some food to eat.

3. You find out if the food is adequate (reward). You need something to eat, but the amount comes as a bonus (or punishment if it fails to make you full). Here, the reward is the satisfaction you get from eating. You just want to find out if is adequate or not, but you will not leave it if you are hungry.

If the reward is pleasant, then you will want to follow the same routine whenever the reminder ensues. In fact, it is for that channel that you eat on a daily basis. Repeat a particular activity several times and it becomes a new habit. The following steps describe a demonstration how you can use these R's in a procedural manner to improve your ways of doing things.

First Step: Set a Reminder for the New Habit

Your friends are likely to come up with two notions if you tell them that you are about to start a new habit. They will suggest that you find a new set of willpower and exercise self-control in all cases. However, those approaches do not guarantee instant success as your friends' opinions may sound. Seeking motivation and remembering to do the new behavior seems the exact wrong technique to use here.

Naturally, your motivation and memory will fail you. That argument is factual because you need something to remind you about the new habit. You lived so far without it, and now you need to adapt to it. Furthermore, a reminder never relies on motivation and does not need you to remember what to do. Instead, it encodes the new trait into the ones you do all the times.

The following example can help you go through this step. In the article, *The Secret to Sticking to the Healthy Habits*, the author narrated how he created a new habit of flossing by doing it after brushing his teeth. In that case, he used the existing habit as a reminder of the new one he adopted. Further, he improvised a way that would prevent him from having to remember the new habit and make the job easier.

The author bought a bowl, filled it with several pre-made flossers, and placed it next to his toothbrush. That arrangement allowed him to floss every moment he reached out for his toothbrush. Here, linking the new convention to the old one and setting up a visible reminder for it allowed him to change. He did not have to remember or seek motivation for it.

You should start making reminders if you only survived through remembrances and motivators. The bottom line, there is no magic that will make you stick to the incoming habits if you cannot set up a system that helps you start them.

Choosing a Reminder

The change will become easier to incorporate if you pick the correct mechanism that reminds you about it. Writing down two lists would be the best approach selecting an appropriate reminder for the incoming practice. The first list should contain the activities you do on a daily basis without fail. Examples here would include:

- Getting in the shower
- Putting the shoes on
- Brushing your teeth
- Flushing the toilet
- Sitting down for supper
- Turning all the lights off before sleeping or leaving the house
- Getting into the bed after dinner

Most items in the above list are the daily health habits. You can use them as reminders for new ones you would to adopt. For example, you could go for, "I meditate for one minute after having my breakfast." In your second list, jot down the things that take place in your life without fail.

Consider the following activities:

- Traffic lights turn yellow, green and red
- You receive text messages and phone calls
- Commercial adverts come on the television
- A song plays in the stereo
- The sun sets in the evening

These lists will comprise a collection of the things you do and respond to each day. They are perfect reminders for any practice you plan to undertake for the first time. Perhaps, you wanted to feel happy. How would achieve it. Expressing your gratitude is one of the proven ways that can boost your happiness.

Using the first list, you could pick one reminder, say *"Sitting down for supper"*, as a cue for saying something you feel grateful for the day. For example, *"when I sit down for supper, I feel grateful for reaching home before the rains."* Such an approach may seem a small behavior, but it can blossom into something that impress you for a long time.

CHAPTER 4 – SELECTING HABITS

Step Two: Select a Habit that is easy to Start

The desire to ring in massive changes in life can catch up with you in a very simple way. You watch incredible transformations of weight loss in the TV and think that you can shed off 30 pounds in the next month. You see an elite athlete on the screen and think that you will jump higher, run faster, kick a ball harder, or box better by tomorrow. You want earn hefty sums, do many things, and get involved in more than one profession.

You are not alone in that line. The problem is, like every other person with the same wishes, you want to accomplish all those wishes the moment you get the desire. That is almost ridiculous because even the athletes and TV programs you want to copy did not become victorious in one day. However, that is understandable because almost every person goes through it. In fact, it is an enthusiastic feeling that people should fancy having. You yearn for acquiring great things in life, and that alone can help you develop habits that will lead you to success. All in all, try to learn that a lasting change requires continual struggle and a result of the daily conventions.

No once–in–a–lifetime transformation can make you victorious overnight. If you want to come up with a different habit and live a happier and healthier life, then adopt the policy that this ebook presents. Start in a small way. Babauta Leo implies the same thing when he says, *"make it look so easy that you find it hard to resist"*. However, the problem many people may find from this suggestion is how small someone should start. Fogg B. J. responds to that matter in perfect manner.

He refers to flossing of the teeth, in which he affirms that anybody interested in that should start by just one tooth. When you start a particular trait, your performance does not count. All you need to show is the ability to stick out to it. With time you will get to the level of pursuance you want as the new behavior becomes consistent. If you acquire Leo and Fogg's concepts in a systematic manner, you will never find difficulties in building the incoming trait. Here is the action step you should follow. Decide what your new habit should become. After which, ask yourself, "How can I make my decision easy to do that I cannot resist it?"

What is the Reward?

Everybody would like to celebrate at the end of his or her struggle. The celebration bit makes them want to do the things that will bring joy to their situations. Since all actions need repetition to become habits, they should reward whenever you practice them. For example, if your goal is to work towards a particular fitness exercise, then you need something to tell yourself at the end of each session. "That was better than what I did yesterday" or "This is a positive result, I am making progress", would some of the best lines to tell yourself each day.

Sometimes the result is so impressive that you find yourself yelling "victory!", "success!", or "I am the champion!" can slip your tongue. The old men warned, "Do not toot your own horn", however, it is understandable that giving yourself some credit is just a way of enjoying the success, and not necessarily boasting. Note that you should only pursue the habits you deem important to you. Rewards may not come by if you do things because other people praised their importance.

What is the Next Step?

From a general point of view, these three R's suit almost all habit. However, there are specific cases that may demand extra work. In some cases, you need to conduct a slight experiment before you grasp the appropriate cue that will remind you to start up a new behavior. That is, you may have to do a bit of thinking before spelling out how to make it too easy to resist. In addition, it is crucial to learn that not all people like rewarding themselves with self-talk. If you belong to that category, then you will take some time to learn it. Everything is a process that requires time.

Daniel Wells

CHAPTER 5 – THE RULES OF EFFECTIVE HABITS

Just like any other practical activity, effectual conventions have regulations. This eBook uses Davenport Barrie's encounter to outline the policies that valid habits follow. Davenport had a client whose body weight recorded in excess of 400 lbs. She had a poor diet that consisted of too many sweets and junk food, and she never bothered to do any physical exercise.

The client found it hard to socialize with other people because she was embarrassed with the way she looked. That lady was 33, but she has never been on a single date. The lady longed to visit Europe, but she could not travel by airline because all the seats in the plane could not accommodate her. In addition, she did not like her job.

Ironically, she had more abilities and talents than many of her workmates. However, the only problem was the fact that she had little to no self-confidence.

'Miraculously,' she underwent the change of her lifetime in a space of two years. Following are the transformations she experienced:

- Lost more than 200 lbs.
- Started physical exercises and weight training on a daily basis
- Began eating healthy delicacies and gave up sweets, junk and processed food
- Pursued her life-long dream by quitting the job she hated for a personal business
- Started a personal blog about losing weight and healthy lifestyle
- Wrote and published a book
- Started dating by engaging in her first relationship
- Networked, socialized and is planned a plane trip to Europe
- Almost covered all her debts

What was her Secret?

It is almost intriguing that the turned her life around in just two years. She became healthy, fit, organized, successful, and attractive. Anyway, how did she manage all that within that time span? Davenport reported that the client allowed him to writer her story. Therefore, it is imperative to borrow the same story to inspire you.

The client's name was Stephanie and she did all those remarkable transformations by herself. Almost everybody find it hard to incorporate new habits into their lives. As such, Stephanie must have faced an uphill task in creating several habits in the two years she struggled to change her life.

If you are interested in knowing how hard adopting a new behavior can get, consider changing a diet. You must come up with a new pattern of shopping, the food selection, the cooking system, the eating program, and the dining out habits. Any of those activities will consume much energy and time.

Daniel Wells

CHAPTER 6 – THE SECRET

For Stephanie to enjoy that prosperity, she must have known something many people do not. However, that may seem an overstatement. This lady just learned the skills for building traits that last. She did not stop until she achieved her goals, which demanded a lot of involvement. While practicing those techniques, Stephanie had to follow some regulations. The following are some of the rules that govern habit creation.

1. Preparation

Unless you plan and prepare yourself, you cannot launch into a new habit. In fact, you should expect failure if you skip this step. You need mental, physical and emotional readiness in order cope up with the incoming behavior. Here, you need to vision the outcomes and plan a system of reminders, support, accountability, and rewards.

2. Build Accountability

Often, people keep their new habit a secret because they do not want to become the laughing stocks if they fail. On the contrary, this eBook cautions that you have a slim chance of succeeding on your behavior if you hide it from others. Success will come your way if you let your friends know about it. You are likely to work hard when they pay attention to you. Therefore, try to look for ways of announcing your incoming behavior before perfecting it.

3. Look for Supporters

One of the primary reasons for informing others about the new character change is to seek their support. Some of them could have experience on the same; while others may be willing to help you develop it. As such, let the people close to you know that you plan to make a change in your life. One of the things you may consider seeking from them in return is their support.

Failure to do that may cause some troubles. If your new habit interrupts their life and you failed to tell them about it, they may retaliate. They could sabotage it and leave you helpless. Being a procedural process, habit creation drains your emotions, time, and energy. For that reason, you need somebody to support you through the struggle.

A FINAL WORD

A habit is any behavior that establishes through repetition. This eBook has outlined that a person's life is a manifestation of his her habits. If you create productive characters, success would come your way with ease. Otherwise, your life is likely to remains the same or even get worse. However, this book has presented six chapters with detailed information on how you can come up with life-transforming traits.

In order to adopt relevant behaviors, you should follow the above steps. There are some factors that underline creation of habits. For example, you need to focus on one goal at a time. Lastly, you must pay attention to the three R's and observe the rules of building habit.

Please Leave a Review

Finally, if you enjoyed this book, please take the time to share your thoughts and post a review on Amazon. It'd be greatly appreciated!

That review and feedback will help me improve the content in my books – and make each and every one more relevant and helpful to you.

Thank you again and good luck!

Daniel Wells